Quilt Notes

Mildred McKinnie developed a unique method for making the triangle units used in the Ocean Waves design. This method eliminates the construction of hundreds of triangle/square units.

Beginning with squares cut the same size, her method creates a unit that when cut creates four triangle units comprised of four triangles each. No matter what size square you choose, you will create the same units, just in different sizes. If using 4" squares, the resulting triangle/square units are 2" finished.

Even though it sounds complicated, it really is so easy it seems impossible. But it works.

Read over the Ocean Waves Made Easy section and refer to it often to create other projects. You might even come up with a few ideas of your own. Once you have tried the method, you will be making waves all the time.

Meet the Designer

Mildred McKinnie

Mildred McKinnie is a farm wife from southern Iowa. As a young child she was taught to sew and quilt by her mother, who spent the winters making quilts. She has enjoyed sewing ever since.

Mildred has always tried to find easier ways to construct her quilt designs. She developed a method of making Ocean Waves units that eliminates cutting all those little triangles that require bias-edge stitching to make triangle/square units.

After perfecting her method, Mildred found that the resulting units could also be used in other designs, such as the Ocean Waves Stars quilt on page 10. Mildred is on a mission to develop more quick-and-easy methods to help quilters find success even when stitching what appear to be difficult blocks.

E-mail: Customer_Service@whitebirches.com

Ocean Waves Made Easy is published by House of White Birches, 306 East Parr Road, Berne, IN 46711, telephone (260) 589-4000. Printed in USA. Copyright © 2004 House of White Birches.

RETAILERS: If you would like to carry this pattern book or any other House of White Birches publications, call the Wholesale Department at Annie's Attic to set up a direct account: (903) 636-4303. Also, request a complete listing of publications available from House of White Birches.

Every effort has been made to ensure that the instructions in this pattern book are complete and accurate. We cannot, however, take responsibility for human error, typographical mistakes or variations in individual work.

ISBN: 1-59217-060-9
1 2 3 4 5 6 7 8 9

STAFF

Editors: Jeanne Stauffer, Sandra L. Hatch
Associate Editor: Dianne Schmidt
Technical Artist: Connie Rand
Copy Editors: Michelle Beck, Sue Harvey, Nicki Lehman
Graphic Arts Supervisor: Ronda Bechinski

Graphic Artists: Debby Keel, Edith Teegarden
Assistant Art Director: Karen Allen
Photography: Tammy Christian, Christena Green, Kelly Wiard
Photo Stylist: Tammy Nussbaum

Ocean Waves Made Easy

Traditional Ocean Waves

The traditional Ocean Waves quilt is not stitched in blocks, but combines Ocean Waves units with whole squares and edge triangles to create the quilt top as shown in photo above and Figure 1.

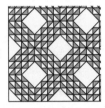

Figure 1
Ocean Waves units are joined with a square in the traditional Ocean Waves quilt.

In the method described in this book, the Ocean Waves units are stitched in a whole new way, and these units are used to create a variety of projects in different ways.

Piecing the triangle units used to create the Ocean Waves unit is quick and easy. Try it to discover how simple making these units can be.

Method Instructions

Before you begin a project, practice the method using some scrap fabrics. Note that the triangle units have bias edges that easily stretch requiring careful handling when joining them in projects.

The size of the square used to create the units may vary. The projects in this book use 4" and 6" squares, but any size square may be used to make different-size units. A 4" square results in 2" finished-size triangle/square units and a 6" square results in 3" finished-size triangle/square units in the completed project.

Refer to the following instructions for making units for all projects in this pattern book.

Making An Ocean Waves Block

1. Cut two 4" by fabric width strips of two different fabrics, one light and one dark.

2. Layer one strip of each fabric with right sides together and press.

3. Subcut the layered strips into 4"-square layered segments. Subcut the remaining strips into 4" square segments. **Note:** *Each block requires six layered squares and six single squares of each fabric.*

4. Using a ¼" seam allowance, sew around all outside edges of six of the layered squares as shown in Figure 2.

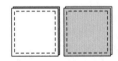

Figure 2
Sew around all outside edges of 6 layered squares.

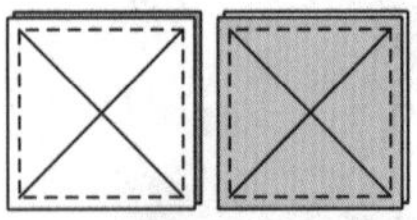

Figure 3
Mark 3 units with an X on the light side and 3 with an X on the dark side.

5. Mark three units with an X on the light side and three with an X on the dark side as shown in Figure 3.

6. Cut along the marked lines from stitching line to stitching line through the marked layer only as shown in Figure 4.

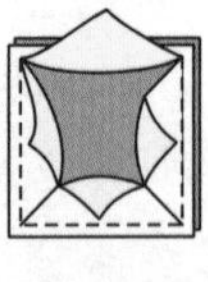

Figure 4
Cut along the marked lines through the marked layer only.

7. Press cut edges open to reveal the pieced units as shown in Figure 5.

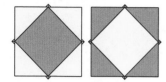

Figure 5
Press cut edges open to
reveal the pieced units.

8. Cut six single squares of each fabric in half on one diagonal to make triangles.

9. Select four triangles to match the center of a pieced unit. Stitch a triangle to two opposite sides of the pieced unit as shown in Figure 6; press seams toward triangles. Repeat on the opposite sides to complete one unit as shown in Figure 7. Repeat to complete three light and three dark units.

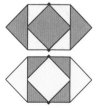

Figure 6
Stitch a triangle to opposite
sides of the pieced unit.

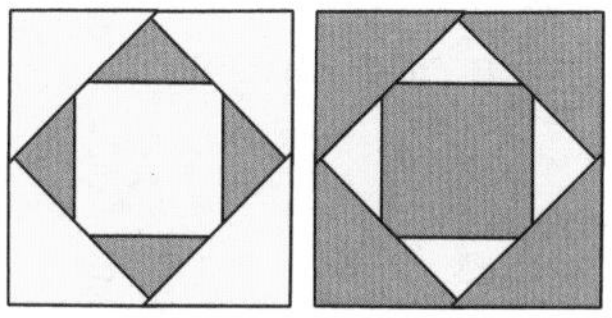

Figure 7
Sew triangles to remaining
sides to complete 1 unit.

10. Carefully mark an X from corner to corner on each pieced unit as shown in Figure 8; cut apart on marked lines, again referring to Figure 8. **Note:** *The way the units are pieced and cut*

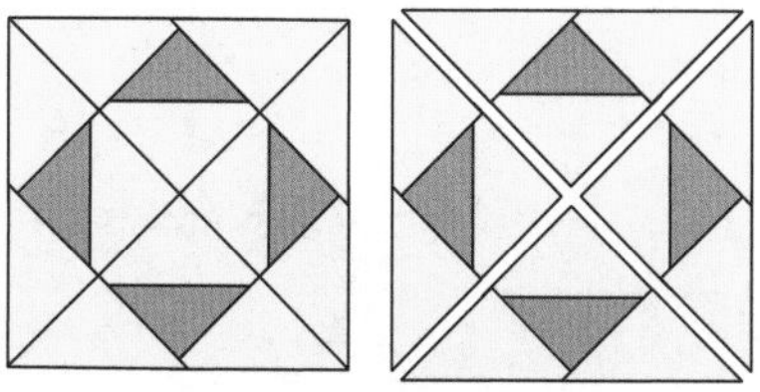

Figure 8
Carefully mark an X from corner to
corner on each pieced unit; cut
apart on marked lines.

allows a ¼" seam between the triangles for future piecing as shown in Figure 9.

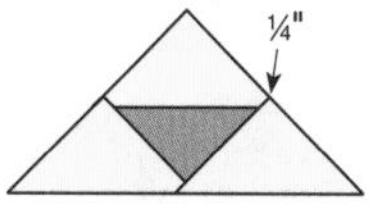

Figure 9
A ¼" seam is included between the
triangles for future piecing.

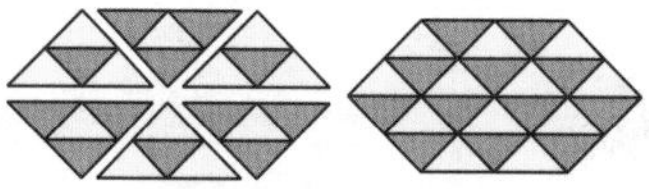

Figure 10
Join 6 units to complete 1
Ocean Waves unit.

11. Join three each light and dark triangle units as shown in Figure 10 to complete one Ocean Waves unit; repeat for four units.

12. Cut four squares light fabric 4⅞" x 4⅞"; cut each square in half on one diagonal to make triangles.

13. Sew a triangle to opposite sides of each Ocean Waves unit as shown in Figure 11; press seams toward triangle.

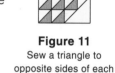

Figure 11
Sew a triangle to
opposite sides of each
Ocean Waves unit.

14. Join four Ocean Waves units to complete one Ocean Waves block as shown in Figure 12; press.

Using Ocean Waves Units in Borders

1. Using the triangle units created through step 10 for the Ocean Waves blocks, join light and dark units, alternating light and dark to create a strip as shown in Figure 13.

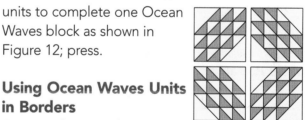

Figure 12
Join 4 Ocean Waves
units to complete 1
Ocean Waves block.

Figure 13
Join triangle units as shown
to make a border strip.

2. Square off ends to make desired length. ■

Classic Ocean Waves Quilt

Use quick-pieced Ocean Waves units to create blocks for this bed-size quilt.

Project Note

This project uses only two fabrics to create the Ocean Waves blocks. To save time, the layered strips may be stitched together along length before cutting the layered squares. This means that two sides of each square remain to be stitched; chain-stitching saves time on this step as well.

Project Specifications

Quilt Size: 93½" x 109½"
Block Size: 16" x 16"
Number of Blocks: 20

Fabric & Batting

- 2⅛ yards brown mottled
- 3⅝" yards tan mottled
- 6½ yards cream tonal
- Batting 100" x 116"
- Batting 100" x 116"

Supplies & Tools

- Cream all-purpose thread
- Basic sewing supplies and tools

Cutting Instructions

1. Cut (24) 4" by fabric width strips each cream tonal and tan mottled. Subcut 12 strips each fabric into 4" square segments. You will need 120 squares.

2. Cut (10) 4⅞" by fabric width strips cream tonal; subcut strips into (80) 4⅞" A squares. Cut each square on one diagonal to make 160 A triangles.

3. Cut eight 3" by fabric width strips tan mottled; join strips on short ends to make one long strip. Subcut strip into two 64½" B and two 85½" C strips.

4. Cut (18) 4½" by fabric width strips cream tonal; join strips on short ends to make one long strip. Subcut strip into two 69½" D, two 93½" E, two 86" H and two 110" I strips.

5. Cut nine 4¾" by fabric width strips brown mottled; join strips on short ends to make one long strip. Subcut strip into two 77½" F and two 102" G strips.

6. Cut (11) 2¼" by fabric width strips brown mottled for binding.

Piecing the Blocks

1. Layer a cream tonal strip right sides together with a tan mottled strip; press to hold.

Classic Ocean Waves
16" x 16" Block

2. Stitch the two strips together along length as shown in Figure 1; repeat for all cream tonal and tan mottled strips.

Figure 1
Stitch a light and dark strip together along length.

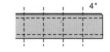

4"

Figure 2
Subcut each stitched strip set into 4" segments.

3. Subcut stitched strip sets into (120) 4" layered squares as shown in Figure 2.

4. Chain-stitch along the unstitched edges of each layered square as shown in Figure 3 to close up both open sides.

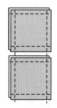

Figure 3
Chain-stitch along unstitched edges of each layered square to close up both open sides.

5. Mark 60 units with an X on the light side and 60 with an X on the dark side and complete 80 Ocean Waves units referring to steps 5–11 in Ocean Waves Made Easy on pages 2 and 3.

6. Sew an A triangle to opposite sides of each Ocean Waves unit as shown in Figure 4; press seams toward A.

Figure 4
Sew an A triangle to opposite sides of each Ocean Waves unit.

Figure 5
Join 4 units to complete an Ocean Waves block.

7. Join four units to complete an Ocean Waves block as shown in Figure 5; press seams in one direction. Repeat for 20 blocks.

Completing the Top

1. Join four Ocean Waves blocks to make a row; repeat for five rows. Press seams in one direction. Join the rows to complete the pieced center; press seams in one direction.

2. Sew B to the top and bottom and C to opposite sides of the pieced center; press seams toward B and C.

3. Sew D to the top and bottom and E to opposite sides of the pieced center; press seams toward D and E.

4. Sew F to the top and bottom and G to opposite sides of the pieced center; press seams toward F and G.

5. Sew H to the top and bottom and I to opposite sides of the pieced center; press seams toward H and I.

Finishing the Quilt

1. Sandwich batting between the pieced top and prepared backing; pin or baste to hold.

2. Quilt as desired by hand or machine. When quilting is complete, remove pins or basting; trim batting and backing edges even with quilted top.

3. Join previously cut binding strips on short ends to make one long strip. Fold binding strip in half along length with wrong sides together; press.

4. Stitch binding to quilt top with raw edges even, mitering corners and overlapping ends. Turn binding to the backside and hand- or machine-stitch in place to finish. ∎

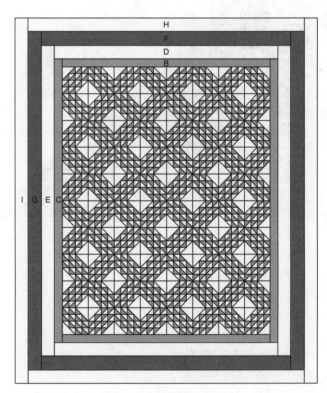

Classic Ocean Waves
Placement Diagram
93½" x 109½"

China Blue Table Set

Ocean Waves triangle units are used to create a place mat and a centerpiece in coordinated solid and print fabrics.

Project Specifications
Centerpiece: 11¼" x 11¼"
Place Mat: 17" x 11¼"

Fabric & Batting
- ⅓ yard white-with-blue print
- ⅔ yard blue solid
- Backing 16" x 16"
- Backing 21" x 16"
- Batting 16" x 16"
- Batting 21" x 16"

Supplies & Tools
- All-purpose thread to match fabrics
- Basic sewing supplies and tools

Preparing Ocean Wave Units

1. Cut two strips each white-with-blue print and blue solid 4" by fabric width.

2. Layer one strip each fabric with right sides together and press.

3. Subcut the layered strips into eight 4" layered squares. Subcut the remaining strips into eight 4" squares each fabric.

4. Using a ¼" seam allowance, sew around all outside edges of the layered squares. **Note:** *Refer to steps 4–10 of Ocean Waves Made Easy on pages 2 and 3 for illustrated method instructions.*

5. Mark four units with an X on the light side and four with an X on the dark side.

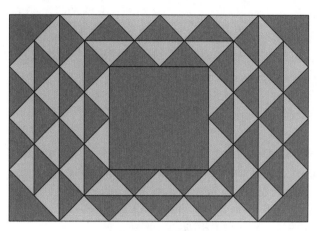

China Blue Place Mat
Placement Diagram
17" x 11¼"

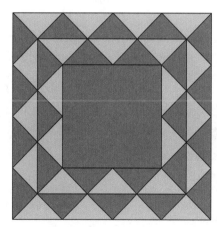

China Blue Centerpiece
Placement Diagram
11¼" x 11¼"

6. Cut along the marked lines through the marked layer only.

7. Press cut edges open to reveal the pieced units.

8. Cut the 4" squares of each color in half on one diagonal to make triangles.

9. Select four triangles to match the center of a pieced unit. Stitch a triangle to two opposite sides of the pieced unit; press seams toward triangles. Repeat on the opposite sides to complete one unit as shown in Figure 1. Repeat to complete four each light and dark units.

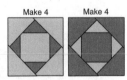

Figure 1
Complete light and dark units as shown.

10. Carefully mark an X from corner to corner on each pieced unit: cut apart on marked lines to complete the pieced units. You will need 14 dark and 16 light triangle units. Set aside two dark units for another project.

Completing Place Mat & Centerpiece Tops

1. Cut two 6⅛" x 6⅛" squares blue solid.

2. Sew a dark triangle unit to opposite sides of one square as shown in Figure 2; press seams toward pieced units.

Figure 2
Sew a dark triangle unit to opposite sides of 1 square.

Figure 3
Sew a light triangle unit to the remaining sides of the square.

3. Sew a light triangle unit to the remaining sides of the square referring to Figure 3; press seams toward pieced units.

4. Sew a light and dark triangle unit together as shown in Figure 4; repeat for four units. Press seams in one direction.

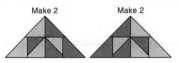

Figure 4
Sew a light and dark triangle unit together.

5. Sew a pieced unit to each side of the pieced center unit to complete a centerpiece top as shown in Figure 5; press seams toward the newly added units. Repeat steps 2–5 to complete a second pieced unit for the place mat center.

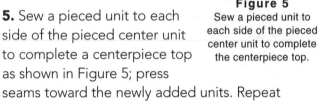
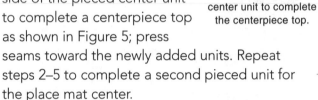

Figure 5
Sew a pieced unit to each side of the pieced center unit to complete the centerpiece top.

6. Join one dark and two light triangle units as shown in Figure 6; press seams away from dark unit. Repeat for two pieced units.

Figure 6
Join 1 dark and 2 light triangle units.

7. Sew a pieced unit to opposite dark sides of the pieced center unit as shown in Figure 7; press seams toward newly added units.

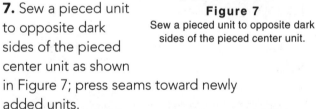

Figure 7
Sew a pieced unit to opposite dark sides of the pieced center unit.

8. Cut two 3¾" x 3¾" squares blue solid; cut each square in half on one diagonal to make triangles. Sew a triangle to each corner of the stitched unit to

Figure 8
Sew a triangle to each corner of the stitched unit to complete 1 place mat top.

complete one place mat top as shown in Figure 8; press seams toward triangles.

9. Sandwich the 21" x 16" batting piece between the place mat top and the 21" x 16" backing piece; pin or baste to hold. Repeat with the centerpiece top and the 16" x 16" batting and backing pieces.

10. Quilt each as desired by hand or machine. When quilting is complete, remove pins or basting; trim edges even.

11. Cut three 2¼" by fabric width strips blue solid for binding. Join strips on short ends to make one long strip. Fold strip in half along length with wrong sides together; press.

12. Pin and stitch binding to edges of quilted projects with raw edges of binding matching raw edges of quilted projects, overlapping binding at beginning and end.

13. Turn binding to the backsides and hand- or machine-stitch in place to finish. ■

Ocean Waves Stars

This star quilt is only one of many creative ways to use these triangle units.

Project Note

Although this is a scrappy-looking quilt, the peach solid and salmon print fabrics are used in the same placement in each block, and dark blue scraps are used for each pinwheel center. The same piecing method used to make the Ocean Waves units is used to create the units needed to piece the star blocks.

Project Specifications

Quilt Size: 83" x 99"
Block Size: 16" x 16"
Number of Blocks: 30

Fabric & Batting

- ½ yard total dark blue scraps or 3 strips 4" by fabric width
- ⅞ yard salmon print
- 1½ yards dark blue print for binding
- 2⅛" yards peach solid
- 3½ yards total assorted scraps or 27 strips 4" by fabric width
- 4 yards white solid
- Batting 90" x 106"
- Batting 90" x 106"

Supplies & Tools

- Neutral color all-purpose thread
- Basic sewing supplies and tools

Cutting Instructions

1. Cut 12 strips peach solid 4" by fabric width for A.

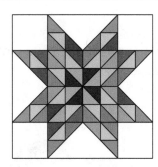

Ocean Waves Star
16" x 16" Block

2. Cut 27 assorted scrap strips 4" by fabric width for B.

3. Cut six strips salmon print 4" by fabric width for C.

4. Cut three strips dark blue scraps 4" by fabric width for D.

5. Cut 14 strips white solid 4½" by fabric width for E and eight strips 9¼" by fabric width for F. Subcut E strips into (120) 4½" E squares. Subcut F strips into (30) 9¼" F squares. Cut each F square in half on both diagonals as shown in Figure 1 to make F triangles.

Figure 1
Cut F squares in half on both diagonals.

6. Cut nine strips peach solid 2½" by fabric width; join strips on short ends to make one long strip.

HOUSE OF WHITE BIRCHES, BERNE, INDIANA 46711   WWW.WHITEBIRCHES.COM

Subcut strip into two 84½" H strips and two 96½" G strips for borders.

7. Cut (10) 5" by fabric width strips dark blue print for binding.

Piecing the Blocks

1. Layer an A strip right sides together with a B strip; press to hold.

2. Stitch the layered strips together along length as shown in Figure 2; repeat for 12 A-B strips.

Figure 2
Stitch an A and B strip together along length.

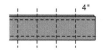

Figure 3
Subcut each stitched strip set into 4" square segments.

3. Subcut the layered strips into (120) 4" layered squares as shown in Figure 3.

4. Chain-stitch along the unstitched edges of each layered square as shown in Figure 4 to close up both open sides.

5. Mark an X on the A peach side of all squares and complete 120 units referring to steps 5–10 in Ocean Waves Made Easy on pages 2 and 3.

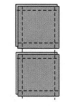

Figure 4
Chain-stitch along unstitched edges of each layered square to close up both open sides.

6. Cut remaining B and all the C and D strips into 4" square segments to total 150 B, 60 C and 30 D squares. Cut each square in half on one diagonal to make 300 B, 120 C and 60 D triangles.

7. Sew a B triangle to opposite sides of all A-B units as shown in Figure 5; press seams toward B.

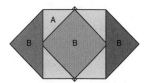

Figure 5
Sew a B triangle to opposite sides of an A-B unit.

8. Sew a C triangle to the remaining sides of 60 A-B-B units to complete an A-B-B-C square as shown in Figure 6; press seams toward C.

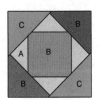

Figure 6
Sew a C triangle to the remaining sides of an A-B-B unit to complete an A-B-B-C square.

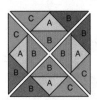

Figure 7
Cut each A-B-B-C square on both diagonals to make 2 A-B-B-C and 2 A-B-B-C reversed units.

9. Cut each A-B-B-C square on both diagonals to make two A-B-B-C and two A-B-B-C reversed units as shown in Figure 7. Repeat for all A-B-B-C squares.

10. Sew a D triangle to the remaining sides of 30 A-B-B units to complete an A-B-B-D square as shown in Figure 8; press seams toward D.

Figure 8
Sew a D triangle to the remaining sides of an A-B-B unit to complete an A-B-B-D square.

Figure 9
Cut an A-B-B-D square on both diagonals to make 2 A-B-B-D and 2 A-B-B-D reversed units.

11. Cut each A-B-B-D square on both diagonals to make two A-B-B-D and two A-B-B-D reversed units as shown in Figure 9. Repeat for all A-B-B-D squares.

12. Sew a B triangle to the remaining sides of the remaining 30 A-B-B units to complete an A-B-B-B square as shown in Figure 10; press seams toward B.

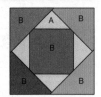

Figure 10
Sew a B triangle to the remaining sides of an A-B-B unit to complete an A-B-B-B square.

Figure 11
Cut each A-B-B-B square on both diagonals to make 4 A-B-B-B units.

13. Cut each A-B-B-B square on both diagonals to make four A-B-B-B units as shown in Figure 11. Repeat for all A-B-B-B squares.

14. Join an A-B-B-D unit with an A-B-B-B unit as shown in Figure 12; repeat for four units. Press seams in one direction. Join the four units as shown in Figure 13 to make a block center; repeat for 15 block centers.

Figure 12
Join an A-B-B-D unit with an A-B-B-B unit.

Figure 13
Join 4 units to make a block center; repeat with 4 reversed units to make a reversed block center.

15. Repeat step 14 with four A-B-B-D reversed units to make a second block center, again referring to Figure 13; press seams in one direction. Repeat for 15 reversed block centers.

16. Sew an A-B-B-C and an A-B-B-C reversed unit to each short side of F to make an F unit as shown in Figure 14; press seams toward F. Repeat for 120 units.

Figure 14
Sew an A-B-B-C and an A-B-B-C reversed unit to each short side of F to make an F unit.

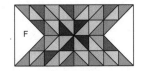

Figure 15
Sew an F unit to opposite sides of 1 block center.

17. Sew an F unit to opposite sides of each block center as shown in Figure 15; press seams toward F units.

18. Sew E to each end of the remaining F units; press seams toward E. Sew the E-F units to the remaining sides of the F-block center units as shown in Figure 16; press seams toward E-F units to complete 30 blocks.

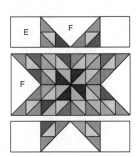

Figure 16
Sew the E-F unit to the remaining sides of the F-block center unit to complete 1 block.

Completing the Top

1. Join five Ocean Waves Star blocks to make a row; repeat for six rows. Press seams in one direction. Join the rows to complete the pieced center; press seams in one direction.

2. Sew G to opposite long sides and H to the top and bottom of the pieced center; press seams toward G and H.

Finishing the Quilt

1. Sandwich batting between the pieced top and prepared backing; pin or baste to hold.

2. Quilt as desired by hand or machine. When quilting is complete, remove pins or basting; trim batting and backing edges even with quilted top.

3. Join previously cut binding strips on short ends to make one long strip. Fold binding strip in half along length with wrong sides together; press.

4. Stitch binding to quilt top with raw edges even using a ¾" seam allowance, mitering corners and overlapping ends. Turn binding to the backside and hand- or machine-stitch in place to finish. **Note:** *This makes a wider bound edge than normal, making the binding look like another narrow border.* ■

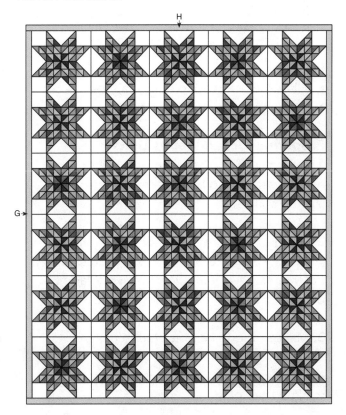

Ocean Waves Stars
Placement Diagram
83" x 99"

Scrappy Bordered Tablecloth

Ocean Waves triangle units create a scrappy border in this simple quilted tablecloth.

Project Specifications
Project Size: 42½" x 42½"

Fabric & Batting
- 36 (6" x 6") squares total light, medium and dark scraps
- 1½ yards navy mottled
- Backing 48" x 48"
- Backing 48" x 48"

Supplies & Tools
- All-purpose thread to match fabrics
- Basic sewing supplies and tools

Preparing Ocean Waves Units
1. Layer two 6" x 6" squares with right sides together and press. Repeat for nine layered squares.

2. Using a ¼" seam allowance, sew around all outside edges of the layered squares. **Note:** *Refer to steps 4–10 of Ocean Waves Made Easy on pages 2 and 3 for method instructions.*

3. Mark an X on one side of each unit.

4. Cut along the marked lines through the marked layer only.

Scrappy Bordered Tablecloth
Placement Diagram
42½" x 42½"

5. Press cut edges open to reveal the pieced units.

6. Cut the remaining 6" x 6" squares in half on one diagonal to make triangles.

7. Stitch a triangle to two opposite sides of the pieced unit; press seams toward triangles. Repeat on the opposite sides to complete one unit as shown in Figure 1. Repeat to complete nine units.

8. Carefully mark an X from corner to corner on each pieced unit; cut apart on marked lines to complete the triangle units. You will need 36 triangle units.

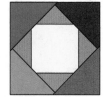

Figure 1
Stitch a triangle to 2 opposite sides of the pieced unit; repeat on the opposite sides to complete 1 unit.

Completing the Pieced Top

1. Cut one 34½" x 34½" square and four 4¾" x 4¾" squares navy mottled. Fold and crease the large square to mark the center.

2. Join nine triangle units to make a strip as shown in Figure 2; press seams in one direction. Repeat for four strips.

Figure 2
Join 9 triangle units.

3. Square off each end of each strip ¼" beyond center points of end units as shown in Figure 3. Strips should measure 34½" long.

Figure 3
Square off each end of each strip ¼" beyond center points of end units.

4. Center and sew a strip to opposite sides of the navy mottled square; press seams toward strip.

5. Sew a 4¾" x 4¾" navy mottled square to each end of the remaining two strips; press seams toward squares.

6. Sew the strips to the remaining sides of the stitched unit to complete the pieced top; press seams toward strips.

Finishing

1. Sandwich batting between the pieced top and prepared backing; pin or baste to hold.

2. Quilt as desired by hand or machine. When quilting is complete, remove pins or basting; trim batting and backing edges even with quilted top.

3. Cut five 2¼" by fabric width strips navy mottled for binding. Join strips on short ends to make one long strip. Fold strip in half along length with wrong sides together; press.

4. Pin and stitch binding to edges of quilted project with raw edges even, overlapping binding at beginning and end.

5. Turn binding to the backside and hand- or machine-stitch in place to finish. ■

Handy Waves

Use this easy technique to create pot holders.

Project Specifications
Pot Holder Size: 6¾" x 6¾" (including binding)

Fabric & Batting
- 4 (4" x 4") squares each light and dark fabrics
- 2 (6¾" x 6¾") squares backing fabric
- 2 (6¾" x 6¾") squares thick cotton batting

Supplies & Tools
- All-purpose thread to match fabrics
- 2 yards brown double-fold bias tape
- Basic sewing supplies and tools

Instructions
1. Layer a light and dark square right sides together; press. Repeat for two layered squares.

2. Using a ¼" seam allowance, sew around all outside edges. **Note:** *Refer to steps 4–7 of Ocean Waves Made Easy on pages 2 and 3 for method instructions.*

3. Mark one unit with an X on the light side and one with an X on the dark side.

4. Cut along the marked lines through the marked layer only.

5. Press cut edges open to reveal the pieced units.

Pot Holder A
Placement Diagram
6¾" x 6¾"

Pot Holder B
Placement Diagram
6¾" x 6¾"

6. Cut the remaining 4" squares in half on one diagonal to make triangles.

7. Referring to the Placement Diagram for positioning, stitch a triangle to two opposite sides of the pieced unit; press seams toward triangles. Repeat on the opposite sides to complete one pot holder top; press seams toward triangles. Repeat to complete two pot holder tops.

8. Sandwich a batting piece between a pot holder top and one backing square; pin or baste to hold. Repeat with second pot holder top.

9. Quilt as desired by hand or machine. When quilting is complete, remove pins or basting; trim edges even if necessary.

10. Bind edges using brown double-fold bias tape, creating a loop on one corner to finish. ■

HOUSE OF WHITE BIRCHES, BERNE, INDIANA 46711   WWW.WHITEBIRCHES.COM